CAN-DO KOSHER!

A Quick and Concise Guide to
Becoming Kosher
(Revised and Expanded)
~ Pocket Edition ~

Chasya Katriela Eshkol

Published in USA by Tovim Press, LLC.

Can-Do Kosher! A Quick and Concise Guide to Becoming Kosher

First published 2016
New expanded pocket edition, published 2018

First Edition Copyright © 2016,
Second Edition Copyright © 2018
by Chasya Katriela Eshkol

All rights reserved. No part of this book may be translated, reproduced, transmitted or stored in a retrieval system, in any form or by any means, be it mechanical, electronic, photocopy, recording or otherwise, without prior written consent from the author and copyright holder.

All kosher certifying agency logos are presented under the "Fair Use Doctrine". Each Agency holds copyright or registered service mark on their own individual seal. These are presented strictly for informational purposes only, and no one agency is endorsed over another.

Cover design and food illustrations copyright Chasya Katriela Eshkol.

ISBN: 978-0-9994786-3-9

Published by Tovim Press, LLC.

CanDoKosher.com

*With Great Thanks and Praise
to Hashem,
this book is dedicated to all
those who truly want to put
everything that they learn
within these pages
into practice.*

*May they have an easy and
pleasant journey to fulfilling
the mitzvah of keeping kosher!*

Table of Contents

Topic	Page
Foreword	vi

Chapter 1

Introduction to Food Types	1
Food Type Chart	1
Meat	3
Parve	10
A Closer Look at Eggs	11
About Fish	13
Naturally Parve Produce	16
Dairy	17

Chapter 2

Separation and Waiting	19
Meat and Dairy	19
Fish and Meat	21
Dairy and Fish (for Some)	22
What Effects Kosher Status	23

Chapter 3

Kosher Supervision	27
Common Hechsher Samples	29
Terms and Definitions	31
Kosher Resources	35
Foods Needing No Supervision	37
General Foods Chart	38
Restaurant/Store Items Chart	39
Foods That Require Supervision	41
Supervised Foods Chart	41

Chapter 4

Preparing to Become Kosher	45
Kashering Chart	49

Chapter 5

The Last Spiritual Step	53
Getting Items Prepared	54
Tavelling Chart	57

Chapter 6

Becoming Kosher "Can-Do" Checklist	59

Foreword

Benefits of Becoming Kosher

Keeping kosher is truly a unique gift that enables you to be more inclusive. You can share food gifts with others, it allows kosher-keeping guests to eat in your home, and best of all, you can have memorable family get-togethers with all of your relatives and friends, whether they keep kosher or not.

Becoming kosher is best done at your own pace. Everyone is different, there is no set time frame, and it can be a fun and rewarding experience. It is said that eating kosher helps the mind to become clearer. Learning the fundamentals is the most important part. "Kashrut",

Foreword

(that which is pertaining to kosher) is a blend between science and religion.

Eating kosher is one of the biggest parts of our Jewish heritage. It is something that defines us as Jews. Many kosher properties have very scientific principles behind them. If you delve deeply into the subject, it is quite fascinating.

On the spiritual level, all laws are derived from the Torah, and Hashem's Wisdom as to what is best for us. These ancient "insights" for a healthy diet, (often termed as "newly discovered" in our times) are always very accurate. Many of the principles can be broken down into charts with a little explanation.

CAN-DO KOSHER!

This little guide is designed to be compact and conveniently carried in a pocket or purse for easy access when you most need it. Full of reference information, you can take it with you to help with shopping for kosher foods, picking out kosher eating places, or preparing new utensils to be ready to use.

It is my hope that this book will help answer most of the questions you may have and prepare you for an exciting new life of eating, drinking and serving kosher food to your friends and family.

L'Chaim!

– *Chasya Katriela Eshkol*

Chapter 1

Introduction to Food Types

In the kosher world, there are 3 types of foods: Meat, Dairy, and *Parve* (Neutral).

Meat	Parve	Dairy
Beef/ Veal	Fruit *	Milk *
Bison/Buffalo	Vegetables *	Half & Half
Lamb/Mutton	Grains	Cream
Venison	Rice	Butter
Chicken	Nuts	Sherbet
Cornish Hens	Seeds	Ice Cream
Duck/Goose	Tofu	Yogurt
Turkey	Honey	Sour Cream
Pigeon/Squab	Eggs*	Soft Cheese
Quail	Fish *	Firm Cheese
Liver *	Vegan Foods*	Hard Cheese*

Raw, unprocessed *parve* foods are always kosher. Meat and dairy must always be kosher certified. Items with * need a bit of explanation, which we'll cover later.

CAN-DO KOSHER!

True vegans will always eat *parve*. Lactose intolerant people will never eat dairy. Those with heart trouble might avoid eating meat. Is it any wonder that the Torah has split our foods into 3 specific groups?

If you fit into any of the above categories, keeping kosher will be no problem at all. For those of us who like to eat all of these, it simply means learning how to deal with each category. Let's break each one down and cover them individually.

Introduction to Food Types

Meat

Meat and meat by-products have several laws. First, it must only be from the kosher species as listed in the table. Also, certain parts of the meat are kosher. Next, all kosher meat is examined for health! Livestock must be farm-raised to ensure their good health, as game animals are known to eat things in the wild that could render them non-kosher. (Nails have been known to be found in deer stomachs!)

The lungs of cattle are checked, and if it is free of most lesions, it is considered kosher. *Sefardim* are stricter with this, as any lesions would deem it non-kosher. Kosher *Sefardi* meat is called "Chalak Bet Yosef" (named for Rabbi Yosef Karo, author of *Shulchan Aruch*, a complex compilation of Jewish laws). *Ashkenazim* will pass a certain type of lesion if it is easily peeled off. When the lungs are smooth, it is deemed "Glatt Kosher". "Chalak" and "Glatt" mean "smooth" in Hebrew and Yiddish respectively. Poultry must be intact with no broken bones or bruises.

Lastly, kosher meat must not contain any blood, due to the Torah's urging that the consumption of any blood is prohibited. This does not include the red juices from the meat. Once it has gone through its kosher preparation, any residue is not considered blood. In fact,

Introduction to Food Types

kosher meat could be eaten raw, although most people wouldn't take the risk of salmonella poisoning!

Traditionally, only the front-half of mammals are used for kosher meat. The back half gets sold off as non-kosher. This is due to the legs containing a forbidden sinew, and other parts containing prohibited fats. (It is only a certain type of fat from very specific areas, so don't freak out if you find some fat in your meat!) It's easier and quicker to sell the entire hindquarters than to painstakingly remove these forbidden parts.

Liver and other specialty meats must be from the kosher species in the list only. The thing with liver is it is saturated with blood, so it goes through a very special braising process to remove it. Most liver is already *kashered* at the meat packing plants.

When purchasing whole poultry, be sure to check the cavities for liver/giblet bags. If found, remove and discard them.

All kosher meat must be "kosher-supervised", as there's a process that animals go through. A *shochet* (kosher slaughterer) uses a special super-sharp knife to quickly slit the throat. If done properly, it's like a barely-felt paper cut, and the animal simply goes to sleep. The knife is examined each and every time to be sure the animal feels no pain. Cruelty to animals is forbidden

Introduction to Food Types

in the Torah. This said, squeamish people might not want to read the next small indented part, but it is an important thing for the kosher consumer to be aware of.

An issue concerning animal cruelty is "White Veal". Anyone who is into animal rights knows the horrendous story about veal calves, specifically "Fancy Milk-Fed Veal".

Unfortunately, this is often the only type of veal that is sold as kosher. A major Rabbi, the head of Star-K, Rav Moshe Heinemann confirmed this with me on the phone several years ago. He explained that these veal calves are raised on non-Jewish farms. When ready for processing, they are sold, and some go to the kosher slaughterhouses. Due to poor health from their growing conditions, they often don't pass the kosher inspections, and are sold off as treifah (non-kosher).

White veal is allowed due to a leniency that they are the end product, and Jews had no part in raising the calves in the hideous conditions to make them white and tender. Those with a conscience about it should not buy it. Now on to happier subjects...

Nowadays, there are a few Jewish companies that raise their meat in a natural way, raised in a field instead of a dark warehouse. These can be found online, and if you are concerned about

Introduction to Food Types

animal welfare, it's worthwhile to look into. (See the next part on eggs as well.)

The nice thing about kosher-supervised meat is there's less for us to do, as it's sold presoaked and salted, removing all blood. Back in the old days, it was up to the housewife to prepare meat by soaking and salting it three times, just to make it kosher. Nowadays it's as easy as putting it in a pot. Enjoy your meat!

CAN-DO KOSHER!

Parve

All raw, unprocessed produce does not need kosher-supervision. Although raw *parve* is inherently kosher, there are still a few things to keep in mind. You may notice that fish and eggs are included in this list of *parve* items. One might think that these would be considered types of meat. We will look at these individually.

Although eggs may come from chickens, they are rather like a "by-products" of the chicken, much like milk from cows and honey from bees. (On an interesting note, honey is yet another *parve* product, and oddly enough, bees aren't even kosher!)

Introduction to Food Types

A Closer Look at Eggs

Cooked or frozen processed eggs, must have certification. Raw eggs, unbroken in the shell are kosher, but of course, they must be from a kosher bird species in the list. There is a way that eggs can be problematic. They cannot be "fertilized", (which are often be sold as a "health food"). This would render them non-kosher.

One must always check eggs when opening them to be sure there are no blood spots. It's as simple as cracking it in a bowl first. It is easiest to use a clear glass bowl. Most of the time cheap eggs pass this test. Most eggs should be okay, as long as the hens aren't around roosters.

Raw eggs in the shell under "kosher-supervision" doesn't mean that they are more humanely-treated, just as with veal calves. The truth is, you don't need to pay more to get a "kosher" egg!

What's the difference between these egg types? Is one better than another?

"*Cage-free*" merely means the hens aren't kept in cages. They may still be kept in a crowded warehouse at all times.

"*Free-roaming*" and "*free-range*" are similar to cage-free. They may have an access door leading to an outside area, that is if they can to make it through the crowd to get there.

"*Pasture-raised*" is perhaps the best, especially if you can find some type of "Certified Humane" label on the package.

Introduction to Food Types

About Fish

For fish to be kosher, it must have fins and scales-period. This rules out all other seafood, such as (scale-less) catfish, crab, snails, turtles, oysters and octopus. Most of these are scavengers or bottom-dwellers, living in polluted or waste waters, and nearly all are known to carry some form of toxins. The Torah considers them non- kosher for good reason.

One can purchase a whole fresh fish, merely wash it well and it's ready to prepare. If it hasn't been gutted, the only thing needed is a visual inspection for worms or other visual parasites in the innards (and sometimes in the gills for certain species).

CAN-DO KOSHER!

Frozen fresh fish should ideally be kosher-certified, unless it is raw fish *only*, with skin visibly attached so that one can see it has scales. In this case it can be purchased without supervision. Here too, it should be rinsed well. Processed fish is a bit trickier. All processed fish must have kosher supervision. This includes raw fresh or frozen fillets, slices or chunks, anything pre-cooked, all canned fish, frozen battered or fried fish, and all prepared sushi.

One may ask the humane question about fish. What is best, farm-raised or wild-caught? There are pros and cons to both. Having been in aquaculture, I can tell you that farm-raised fish (unlike

Introduction to Food Types

chickens and cattle) cannot be raised in crowded or dirty conditions. Not only does it promote disease, but fish will simply not grow. They only reach the size that their environment allows. Diet is the key, and if fish have good quality feed, they'll be healthier and better for you. If not, the opposite may be true.

As for wild-caught fish, they can have their own problems. Seemingly, they should be healthier and better for you, but over-fishing, mercury absorption, and pollution are all factors as well. There's no straight answer as far as humane treatment of fish goes. One must inquire about the company that sells or produces the fish to be sure.

CAN-DO KOSHER!

Naturally-Parve Produce

Fresh, raw produce has one criterion—it must be checked for bugs, since these are not kosher. Therefore, we must take precautions. This is especially true for leafy veggies and produce with cracks and intricate parts. Those to pay extra attention to are broccoli, cauliflower, berries, lettuce, spinach, parsley and the like. It's easiest to check them in sunlight.

Produce that is processed in any way, such as canned, cooked, pureed, or breaded, must all be kosher-certified.

If produce is frozen, plain and without any other ingredients, it may be kosher without certification. One should still check on items as mentioned for bugs.

Introduction to Food Types

Dairy

Milk from sheep or goats must be kosher-certified. There is a leniency with cow's milk in that the USDA regulates it so heavily, that the government is like the kosher supervisor. This is true only in the USA. One must have kosher-certified cows' milk anywhere else in the world. Regardless of this fact, kosher-certified milk is readily available in the USA, and perhaps even better to buy. All other dairy items, even if made with cows' milk, must be kosher-supervised.

A higher-level *kashrut* standard of dairy is "Chalav Yisrael", where milk is supervised by a Jew from the time it came from the cow to processing. It is said to have spiritual benefits, especially for children.

Cheese has its own issues, especially hard cheese. One might think of hard cheese as being solid. Actually, "hard cheese" is akin to "hard liquor", in that it has been "aged" for 3 or more months and tends to cling to the teeth more. Hard cheeses are Parmesan, Romano, Sharp Cheddar, and some types of Swiss. Kosher companies will often state on a package if they're "Aged over 3 Months".

This isn't just a sales propaganda. For those in the know, it means it has the "hard cheese" status, which we talk about later. All other dairy is considered "soft", including firm or medium cheeses.

Chapter 2

Separation and Waiting

There are certain combinations of foods that can never be eaten or served together according to Torah law. This means having separate plates, utensils and cookware. We will cover these forbidden combinations below.

Meat and Dairy

These will never be eaten together due to Torah Law. That only means one must come up with kosher alternatives, like soy cheese on a beef burger, or vegan pepperoni on a real cheese pizza.

With the explosion of vegan foods

CAN-DO KOSHER!

today, it has made it easy for Jews to "mix" foods in a permitted way! Meat is greasy, and tougher than dairy. Whereas one could technically eat dairy, then some *parve*, then have meat (with the exception of hard cheese), one can never eat meat and then have dairy.

This is the general custom of the majority of Jews. Unless your family has a handed-down tradition of waiting less time to eat dairy after meat, you should keep the normal 6-hour waiting period before eating dairy.

(It should be noted that this holds true for hard cheese, as one must wait 6 hours between hard cheese and meat.)

Separation and Waiting

Fish and Meat

Another pair that cannot be mixed is fish and meat. The Sages say there is a risk of health problems when they are combined. Judaism is a religion of life and health, so if there is anything that is a risk to one's health, it is not allowed.

Fortunately, that does not mean one cannot have them at the same meal. One can eat fish on separate plates, eat or drink a bit of *parve* in between (anything other than fish) to clear it away, then eat meat. This works the opposite way as well. One can have meat, eat *parve*, then fish. They just can't be eaten mixed-together.

CAN-DO KOSHER!

Dairy and Fish

Some Jews such as certain groups of *Chassidim* and *Sefardim*, don't mix fish and dairy for the same exact reason as fish and meat. If there's any doubt about health issues, they prefer being strict.

Many *Ashkenazim* do combine them, as with the famous combination of cream cheese and lox on bagels. Some allow fish to be combined with butter only.

The abstinence of mixing fish and dairy is more a tradition than Jewish law. It was also written by Rabbi Yosef Karo about the combining of fish and dairy, although many hold this was a typo meant to say "meat and fish", not "dairy and fish". This is the reason that some combine them and others don't.

Separation and Waiting

What Effects Kosher Status

Meat and dairy are considered "opposite gender" foods. Since meat and dairy can't be mixed, this means having separate dish sets, silverware and cookware. Never can they be used together, cross-contaminated, or washed together.

If one has a dishwasher, it should be designated as either meat or dairy. The same holds true for ovens, and anything that cooks or processes foods. Ovens can be easily *kashered* or made kosher. Ideally, they should not be *kashered* back and forth between dairy and meat to avoid confusion.

If one had no other choice and needed to bake a meat item in a dairy oven (or vice versa) items can be completely double-wrapped in foil, (for microwaves double wrapped with plastic wrap). This works for totally non-kosher ovens and microwaves too, such as at a school or work place. It is an alternative if you must visit any non-kosher place like a relative who may not keep kosher. Just be sure to eat items on a disposable plate.

If one likes to be strict, they can have a third set of dishes and cookware for *parve*, but it is not totally necessary.

Some Jews have separate cookware just for fish, but this is more of a rare family tradition. Most often, fish can be cooked in meat or dairy cookware, as

Separation and Waiting

long as it's completely clean of meat (or dairy if tradition dictates separation).

Ideally, one should color-code all their cookware, dishes and utensils, or at least make them distinct and easy to tell apart at a glance. One can also use special kosher stickers just for the purpose. This helps prevent mix-ups.

In the event of a mix-up or any questionable kosher situation, contact your "LOR" (Local Orthodox Rabbi), who is generally an expert in the field. He will be happy to help. No question is considered "a stupid question".

There are a few things that can affect the kosher status of food or utensils. Heat is the main culprit. If a hot meat pot were set down on a dairy plate, it could possibly make it non-kosher. However, if a drop of milk landed in a hot meat stew, it is okay because it's less than 1/60th of the stew. (This rule is only good in case of an accident.)

Aside from heat, saltiness and "sharpness" can also affect foods. Examples of "sharp" foods are pickles, hot peppers, raw onions or garlic, and anything with a salty brine or vinegar. If one cut an onion with a dairy knife, it becomes dairy, and can't be used on meat. Sharpness has the same effect as heat.

In the event of a mix-up and a utensil's kosher status is in doubt, set it aside 24 hours before asking about it. This may allow it to be *kashered* and saved.

Chapter 3
Kosher Supervision

Why does kosher food need it? Kosher certification assures us that the foods are at the highest standard, as well as just being kosher.

If it were up to the government to determine food "cleanliness", just take a look at the FDA's list of *Allowable Food Defects*. I always found their "Citrus Juice" listing a bit unsettling:

"5 or more Drosophila and other fly eggs per 250 ml or 1 or more maggots per 250 ml."

(One or more *maggots*?! Not one or *less*?)

Kosher consumers are not allowed to eat these abominable types of things, so supervision helps ensure that there are no flies doing the backstroke in our juice.

Kosher-supervised food packages almost always have what is called a "hechsher" or a kosher certification symbol on them. This does not mean just a letter "K", which may or may not be kosher. Some *hechsherim* are more trusted than others. A reliable *hechsher* is the key to making sure your food is completely kosher and has lived up to all the Torah laws. A fundamental of keeping kosher is learning what a *hechsher* can tell you by just a glance. You can see if a product is dairy, meat or *parve*, and possibly if it has been made with dairy or meat equipment. Samples of some common trustworthy *hechsherim* are on the opposite page.

Kosher Supervision

The above samples are not all-inclusive, as there are many more, but this shows several of the most common ones. Any products with these are definitely kosher. If one sees a questionable *hechsher*, it can be described to an Orthodox Rabbi (they know reliable *hechsherim*) or one can call and ask a trustworthy *kashrut* agency.

One mustn't confuse the various logos for vegan products with a *hechsher*. Just because a product says it is vegan, vegetarian, organic, all-natural, GMO-free, or the like, it doesn't mean it is guaranteed kosher. Just know that all flavored, cooked or processed foods need certification.

How do you tell more about a product from the *hechsher*? Often, there are accompanying letters or phrases next to a symbol. These are the terms and definitions:

Kosher Supervision

- **MEAT/Glatt/Chalak/Basar/ בשר:** The product contains meat or some form of it. It cannot be used with dairy.

- **ME/Meat Equipment:** The product was prepared or cooked in utensils that had been used for meat. There are no actual meat ingredients, but it still can't be used directly with dairy. One can eat or drink *parve* in between and then have it. Items like a cake baked in an oven used for meat can be served at a dairy meal, but just not on dairy plates.

- **P:** Logic would dictate that this is *parve*, but actually, a "P" stands for "Kosher for Passover" or "Kasher for Pesach".

- **[Symbol] /PARVE/PAREVE/ פרווה:** A lone *hechsher* with nothing else, or with "*parve*" or "*pareve*" means that it is *parve* with no dairy or meat added. (The three main soft drink companies are supervised, as are many beers, but a *hechsher* doesn't always appear on them.)

- FISH: Most often an item with fish ingredients will have "fish" with the *hechsher*. Some do not, so read the ingredients carefully for Worcestershire sauce, marshmallows, kosher gelatin, and margarines with omegas in them. Yes, it's *parve*, but these fish-based items can't be used directly with meat.

- DE/Dairy Equipment: The product has been prepared or cooked in utensils that had once been used for dairy. Even though there is no actual dairy ingredient, it can't be used or combined with meat. It may be served at a meat meal (as for desserts such as sorbet), but not put on meat plates. One should eat or drink a bit of *parve* in between them. At one time, the OU listed "DE", but later opted to list "D" instead. Unfortunately, this lead to confusion at times. If in doubt, read the ingredients.

- D/DAIRY/Chalav/Cholov/ חלב:
This is made with dairy or some form of it. Some ingredients that are dairy derivatives are whey (originally a cheese-making by-product) and lecithin. This makes some "non-dairy" products, actually dairy, such as whip topping, margarine, coffee creamer, and even many brands of vegan products. There

CAN-DO KOSHER!

are further designations for dairy products:

Chalav Stam meaning "plain dairy", which is normally supervised dairy, or milk that has some or no supervision.

Chalav Yisrael ("Cholov Yisroel" for *Ashkenazim*) is milk watched by a Jew from the time it left the cow to final packing.

Bishul Yisrael and **Pat Yisrael** ("Pas Yisroel" for *Ashkenazim*) are terms used to indicate that food has been cooked (*bishul*) or baked (*pat*) by a Jew.

"Yashan" ("Yoshon" for *Ashkenazim*) means that the harvested grain (of the Five Israeli grains) used in the product have sprouted before the 2nd day of Passover, fulfilling the *mitzvah* or law mentioned in *Vayikra* (Leviticus) 23:14.

Kosher Supervision
Kosher Resources

Whenever you are just starting out, it is helpful to have a list of resources to turn to. Today with smart phones, some of these can be found as apps as well as on a computer. The Star-K, cRc, OU and OK all have phone apps.

The following are found online...

A great resource for any *hechsher* or *kashrut* question, is the Star-K Kosher Hotline at 410-484-4110. They are based in Baltimore, MD and are open 9 AM-5 PM Monday-Thursday, Eastern Time. Fridays 9 AM-2:30 PM.

They also have a chat and email contact on their website if you go to: https://www.star-k.org/contact.

CAN-DO KOSHER!

Another good resource is the cRc (Chicago Rabbinical Council) which has an app called the "cRc Kosher Guide", which shows trustworthy *hechsherim*, as well as lists of kosher items. This app can be found at: http://www.crcweb.org/mobile_apps.php.

There is also a page where you can print out a very nice card to carry around in your wallet that has all the most reliable h*echsherim* from around the country and all over the world: http://www.crcweb.org/kashruscard.pdf.

KOSHER

Foods Needing No Supervision

Yes, there are foods that actually do not need supervision! On the next two pages are cheat charts showing items that don't need a *hechsher* or kosher supervision. The catch is that they can only contain the food mentioned in the entry and cannot contain any other ingredients or additives. They must be 100% pure and without flavorings, or colorings. The only exceptions are vitamins added to milk or flour, which are in such a tiny quantity that it doesn't affect the flavor.

It still doesn't hurt to find a certified product, but if you need an item and can't find one with a *hechsher*, these will suffice. (See conditions listed after charts.)

CAN-DO KOSHER!

Foods Needing No Supervision		
Meat	Parve	Dairy
None	Plain Bottled Waters	Cows' Milk
	Plain Bagged Ice	
	Pure Salt (can be Iodized)	
	Granulated White Sugar	
	Pure Baking Soda	
	Pure Dry Cocoa	
	Pure Coffee and Tea Bags	
	All Pure Flours	
	Raw Legumes	
	Whole Grains & Rice	
	Pure Raw Oatmeal	
	Plain Dry TVP	
	Raw Seeds	
	Raw Nuts	
	Raw Popcorn Kernels	
	Raw Eggs in Shell	
	Whole Raw Fish	
	Fresh Raw Produce	
	Pure Leaf Salads in Bags	
	Fresh Whole Herbs	
	Whole Raw Onions	
	Whole Raw Garlic	
	Raw Frozen Fruit	
	Raw Frozen Veggies	

Foods Needing No Supervision
Conditions for the listed items include:

Bagged fresh leafy vegetables or plain mixed-greens salad must have 3 handfuls removed and checked for bugs.

Frozen fruit may also contain its own pure fruit juice, but no other additives.

Problematic frozen vegetables that can contain bugs, such as broccoli and asparagus, should be checked for bugs.

Instant or whole-bean coffees cannot be decaffeinated.

Non-decaffeinated plain tea leaves in bags only without added flavorings.

Bottled waters, including spring, seltzer, and purified water, must be unflavored.

Raw nuts can be unshelled and chopped.

CAN-DO KOSHER!

Items Bought in Restaurant or Stores
Fountain, bottled, or canned Coca-Cola
Fountain, bottled, or canned Pepsi
Fountain, bottled, or canned Sprite
Fountain, bottled, or canned 7-Up
Fountain, bottled, or canned Mountain Dew
Fountain, bottled, or canned Dr. Pepper
Beer (Plain, No Special Flavors)
Plain (Unflavored) Hot Coffee
Plain (Unflavored) Hot Tea
Plain Hot Water
Plain Water with or without Ice
Crushed Ice

The above items can be ordered from hotels, restaurants, stores, and cold vending machines, only under these conditions:

All drinks, (especially hot drinks), must be in a disposable (preferably paper) cup.

Soft drinks must be the brand-names listed above only (which are certified).

Sugar packets can be used, but creamers must have certification. Plain milk may be used if it's straight from a carton.

Foods That Require Supervision

Foods That Require Supervision

The next charts contain foods that must have kosher supervision, and therefor do need a *hechsher*. Some items like soft drinks, beer and cereals may not always display a *hechsher*, but are actually under kosher supervision. These products must be checked into on the various *kashrut* agency lists given previously in the "Resources" section.

Foods That Require Supervision		
Meat	Parve	Dairy
Raw/Cooked Meat	Raw/Cooked Fish Fillets	Goats Milk and Cheese
Raw/Cooked Poultry	Canned Fruits and Veggies	Sheep Milk and Cheese
Cold Cuts/	Dried Fruits	Cream
Lunchmeat	Raisins	Half & Half
Chicken Fat	Margarine	Butter/Margarine
Sausages	Canned Fish	Yogurt
Hot Dogs	Vegan Meat	Vegan Meat
Jerky	Vegan Cheese	Vegan Cheese
Frozen Snacks	Frozen Snacks	Frozen Snacks

CAN-DO KOSHER!

Foods That Require Supervision		
Meat	**Parve**	**Dairy**
Chicken Nuggets	Breaded Fish /Fish Sticks	Sour Cream and Dips
Chicken Cutlets	Sushi and Seaweed	Puddings and Custards
Ground Meat	Egg Substitute	Candy Bars
Meat Gravy	Soft Drinks	Hot Cocoa
Meat Broth	Drink Mixes	Drink Mixes
Canned Meat Soup	Any Canned Soups	Dairy/Cream-Based Soups
Soup Mix	Soup Mix	Soup Mix
Side Dish Mix	Dry Mixes	Dry Mixes
Vacuum-Packed Meals	Vacuum-Packed Meals	Vacuum-Packed Meals
Frozen Meals	Frozen Meals	Frozen Meals
Meat Restaurants	Vegan Restaurants	Dairy Restaurants
Liver	Pasta/Noodles	Pizza
Tongue	Pie Crusts	Pie Crusts
Heart	Pies	Pies
Sweetbreads	Cookies	Cookies
	Crackers	Crackers
	Cakes	Cakes
	Bread, Matza and Tortillas	English Muffins

Foods That Require Supervision

Foods That Require Supervision	
Parve	**Dairy**
Roasted Nuts/ Seeds	Any Kind of Cheese
Candy/Fruit Leather	All Cheese Spreads
Non-Dairy Whip Cream	Whipped Topping
Fruit Sorbet/Juice Bars	Sherbet
Parve Ice Cream	Ice Cream
Smoothies	Caramel Syrups
Bottled or Canned Juices/Fruit Drinks	Diet and Nutritional Shake Supplements
Drink Enhancers	Energy Drinks
Grape Juice	Chocolate Milk
All Wines	Condensed Milk
Vegetable Oil	Evaporated Milk
Pickled Fish	Creamed Herring
Cereals/Granola & Nutrition Bars	Cereals/Granola & Nutrition Bars
Breading Crumbs	Pancakes/Waffles
Pretzels	Pretzels
French Fries/ Potato Chips	Spicy Fries/Crunchy Cheese Snacks
Salad Dressing/Mayo	Salad Dressing Mixes
Pickles/Condiments	Doughnuts
Gelatin/Marshmallows	
Flavored Beverages	
Chewy/Liquid Medicine, Cough Drops & Vitamins	

CAN-DO KOSHER!

Of course, this isn't an all-inclusive list, but gives one the idea of the vast majority of kosher-certified foods that are out there. Any specialty foods like meat, cheese and bread that can't be found in stores can be ordered online.

Kosher-certified restaurants can be found by contacting a local *kashrut* agency. Don't be misled by establishments saying they are "Kosher-Style", as they are *not* kosher.

One should note that flavored liquid or chewable medicines, cough drops, and vitamins must be kosher-certified. They can be dairy or contain non-kosher ingredients. Unless there is no kosher equivalent available and/or it's life-threatening, one should stick to a kosher-certified version.

Chapter 4

Preparing to Become Kosher

Now that you know how to tell what products are kosher, we move on to what to do in your home, and how to prepare for it.

This process is much like preparing for Passover. Here we have a primer that should take care of most, if not all issues. The first thing to do is to go through all of your food to determine if there is anything that can be kept. Refer to the previous "Kosher Supervision" chapter to determine what foods to keep and what to donate to non-Jews or a non-kosher food pantry.

CAN-DO KOSHER!

Before starting the actual *kashering* process, you must also determine what can be *kashered* and what should go to the thrift store. Use the *kashering* charts on the next few pages to see what can and cannot be *kashered* and kept.

A helpful step is pre-designating the areas of your kitchen to know where to store the different items. One bank of cabinets should have meat plates and cookware, another should have dairy. Some even like to have a third area for *parve* items. Get your color-coded stickers, markers or nail polish ready for after the next two steps. Before you start, put a sticky note on each cabinet until you get used to your new system!

Preparing to Become Kosher

The day before *kashering*, clean all areas where food is stored or cooked. Thoroughly scrub the kitchen sink(s), rinse well, and let sit unused 24-hours. This is the procedure for everything in the kitchen, with exception of a fridge and dishwasher. It is helpful to have a large stock pot on hand, just for *kashering*. Bonus- this *kashering* pot can be used for Passover too!

It may be possible to *kasher* existing kitchen items so that they will become kosher. There are a few guidelines to follow. One must know the items that can be *kashered*. Anything made of metal (without grooves, blades, crevices, non-stick coating or paint) can be *kashered*. Items are *kashered* in the manner that they were used. Pots are usually *kashered* by boiling, baking pans by baking. If an item's history is unknown, it gets the strictest heat. Glass used cold is *kashered* in a unique way by *Ashkenazim*. *Sefardim* only wash them well, since they hold glass doesn't absorb.

On the next few pages are cheat charts of items and how they're *kashered*. If in doubt, ask an expert in the field, your LOR.

Items with * are of mixed opinions, and your Rav should be consulted. The following methods are used after the cleaning and 24-hour sitting period is over. (It's advisable to line your floor with towels because *kashering* can be a messy business.)

Preparing to Become Kosher

Item	Kashering Method
Porcelain Sinks * (Cold-use only for *Sefardim*)	Pour boiling water over entire surface.
Tile, Recycled Glass/Rock Composite Counters	Not *kasherable*.
Stainless Steel Sinks/Counters, Polished Smooth Natural-Rock Counters	Pour boiling water over entire surface.
Formica/Laminate Countertops *	Some say not *kasherable*, others say do as above.
Countertops of Corian and Wood	Can be *kashered* only by professional sanding.
Gas Stove Top Burners	Scour grates and burner heads. Either put grates in the oven through a Self-Cleaning Cycle, or flip the grates and drape foil over them, then turn burners on High for 20 minutes.
Coil Burner Electric Stoves	Turn on High until coils glow red for 10 minutes.
Smooth/Flat/Ceramic-Glass Cook Tops * (Most hold these cannot be *kashered*)	Those that do, do as Coil Burners. *Sefardim* also pour boiling water over top to *kasher* the rest.
Self-Cleaning Gas and Electric Ovens	Run oven through Self-Cleaning Cycle, racks in.
Non-Self-Cleaning Gas and Electric Ovens	Turn setting to Broil for at least 1-hour.

CAN-DO KOSHER!

Item	Kashering Method
Refrigerators	No need, clean well.
Dishwasher * (Many hold these cannot be *kashered*)	Those that do, put a caustic cleaner such as cleanser in dispenser. Run through a cycle. Repeat 3 times.
Microwave * (A few hold these cannot be *kashered*)	Those that do, fill a disposable bowl with water, swish in a bit of dish soap. Microwave at full power for 6 minutes or until steamy. Wipe out with paper towels.
Toaster Ovens, Toasters, Warming Trays, Crock Pots, Teflon/Non-Stick, Painted, Porcelain Enamel Pots/Pans	Cannot be *kashered*. Find them a new home.
Outdoor Grills, Stove-Top Built-In Grills	Not easily *kashered*, but possible. Racks should be replaced with new ones, and grill fired up as high as possible for about 1-hour.
Non-Stick Indoor Grills, Waffle/ Sandwich Makers	Cannot be *kashered*. Find them a new home.

Preparing to Become Kosher

Item	Kashering Method
Blenders, Choppers, Food Processors	Cannot be *kashered*. Find them a new home.
Uncoated Metal Frying Pans * Most Knives * (See Utensils for Butter Knives)	Some hold these items can't be *kashered*. Others hold use boiling water as below. Some hold that Frying Pans (handles removed) can be put through a Self-Cleaning Oven Cycle. Ask your LOR.
Uncoated Metal Pots and Pans	*Kasher* by immersing in a pot of boiling water so that every part of it has made contact with it, then immediately plunge into cold water.
Uncoated Metal Baking Sheets, Muffin Tins, and Cake Pans	Probably best to buy new, but they can be put through a Self-Cleaning Cycle (if they make it).
All Items Made of Porcelain, China, or Stoneware	Cannot be *kashered*. Find them a new home.
Corelle, Arcorac, Duralex, or Pyrex Dishes only *	Some hold not *kasherable*. Those that do, *kasher* in boiling water, then rinse in cold water as for Uncoated Metal Pots.

CAN-DO KOSHER!

Item	Kashering Method
Plastic or Silicone Items	Cannot be *kashered*. Find a new home or buy new.
Drinking/Cold-Used Only Glasses	*Sefardim*- wash well! *Ashkenazim*- submerge in bucket 24 hours 3 consecutive times, change water each time.
Metal Utensils, Butter Knives and Silverware Note: For all other Knives, see the previous page.	*Kasher* by immersing in a pot of boiling water so that every part of it has made contact with it, then immediately plunge into cold water.

Once items have been *kashered*, it's a good idea to wash them well with dish soap, as there is usually a leftover residue on them. Note that stovetop centers are considered not kosher. Items should not be set there.

Once your items are kosher, they are ready for their next spiritual phase called *tavelling* or immersing. All new items that have not been made in Israel or by a Jew goes through the process as well.

Chapter 5
The Last Spiritual Step

The last element in preparing to use your kosher kitchen is to finalize the "Jewishness" of your cookware and dishes. This is done for first-time *kashered* items, and for all newly purchased items made outside of Israel. If you got an item from a non-Jew, new or used, it should be *tavelled* too.

"Tavelling" (*Ashkenazim* may say "Toivelling") or immersing an item only needs to occur the one initial time. (*Kashering* on the other hand may be done more than once, such as if an item has accidentally become non-kosher or it's being made kosher for Passover use.)

CAN-DO KOSHER!

The act of *tavelling* is accomplished by dipping items in a natural body of water, or a kosher Jewish *mikvah*. It is such a big *mitzvah* that a blessing is said before you do it!

Tavelling "sanctifies" objects to turn them into a "Jewish" item. (Converts to Judaism go through this same process!)

If you have never done this to your items before, here's your chance to make them spiritually special!

∞∞∞∞∞∞∞∞∞

Getting Items Prepared

Once old items are kosher, they must be cleaned from the *kashering* residue. For new items, make sure they are free of any stickers or labels. If there are

Spiritual Preparation

stubborn stickers or gum residues, take a bit of Pine-Sol on a paper towel, soak the area, and let it sit awhile. The sticky residue should easily come off, then wash it well.

Tavelling is not needed for items made of plastic, Styrofoam, rubber, or silicone, and disposable items that are only used once.

It is only necessary for items that actually touch food. Some items require the *bracha* (blessing), others do not. Those with * have mixed opinions. All metal or glass items definitely get the *bracha*. Items that are questionable, such as stoneware, are immersed after an item that needs a *bracha* in order to get its own well-deserved place in the Jewish home.

CAN-DO KOSHER!

If needed, ask a rabbi where the nearest "keilim mikvah" is, or go to a natural body of water. Bring a lot of towels and a *siddur* (Jewish prayer book). If you have a lot of silverware you can bring a plastic or wire basket to immerse all of them at once. Make sure the holes or slits are small enough so no items fall out. More *tavelling* tips after the charts.

Once you arrive at the *mikvah* or shore, get your items accessible. Say the *bracha* from a *siddur*. Next, after the blessing, wet your hands and then entirely submerse each item one by one so that every part has touched the water. *Do not talk until you are done!* On the next pages are cheat charts on *tavelling*.

Spiritual Preparation

* Questionable items don't get a *bracha*.

Items to Tavel	With A Bracha
Metal Silverware, Any Metal Utensils Touching Food	Yes
Drinking Glasses. Metal-Lined Thermos. Glass, Corelle, Duralex, Pyrex, Arcorac Dishware	Yes
Slow-Cooker Crocks, Stoneware, Earthenware, China, Porcelain *	*Tavel* items that get a *Bracha* first, and dip this in between.
Glass Crock Pot Lids, Metal or Glass Pot Lids	Yes
Pots, Pans, Metal or Glass Bakeware and Coffee Pots	Yes
Painted, Porcelain, or Non-Stick Cookware *	*Tavel* items that get a *Bracha* first, and dip this in between.
Graters, Knives, Food Processor and Blender Blades	Yes

CAN-DO KOSHER!

Items to Tavel	With A Bracha
Grill Racks, Electric Grills, Coffee Urns, Sandwich and Waffle Makers	Yes (Be sure to let electrical appliances dry out 2 weeks)
Toaster, Toaster-Ovens, Glass or Metal Refrigerator Shelves	NO NEED TO TAVEL!
Oven Racks and Toaster Oven Racks Never Touching Food	NO NEED TO TAVEL!
Oven Racks and Toaster-Oven Racks That Food is Placed On Directly	Yes

If *tavelling* items in a basket, gently place it in the water and shake up and down so that all parts of the items contact the water. Pack up *tavelled* items in towels and bring back home to wash one last time. Then they can be put in their final destinations.

Chapter 6

Becoming Kosher "Can-Do" Checklist

Follow the Can-Do Checklist below and scratch each item off the list as you do it.

- ✡ Go through all your foods and eliminate the ones that are not kosher, keep any that are. Set these aside for future use.

- ✡ Designate what areas will be meat, dairy, and if needed, *parve*. Be aware that the burnerless center area of a stovetop is always considered non-kosher, especially when hot.

- ✡ Go through all of your cookware, dishes, bakeware, utensils, etc. to see what can be *kashered* and what can't. Anything that can't be *kashered* can be donated to a thrift store.

CAN-DO KOSHER!

✡ If you are *Ashkenazi*, cold-*kasher* your glasses. (This can be done well in advance.)

✡ Purchase a new large stock pot to be used for *kashering* only. (It comes in handy for Passover!)

✡ Go food shopping if desired. Look for items with a *hechsher*. You may be surprised at how much is kosher-certified!

✡ Purchase any needed cookware or items that you don't have or need to replace. It is best to color-code items as to type for easy at-a-glance identification. (Examples of color-coding are Red=Meat; Green=Parve; Blue=Dairy.)

✡ Clean the kitchen thoroughly and let it sit 24 for hours or longer. (This is a great time to take a day trip or go out to eat!)

"Can-Do" Checklist

- ✡ Starting to *kasher*: *Kasher* the Stove top first. Usually it's as easy as turning on the burner.

- ✡ Once kosher, fill up the stock pot in the bath tub and set on burner to boil. Be sure you can lift it easily.

- ✡ Put towels down, this is a messy business. *Kasher* the kitchen sink. Refill and repeat, until all the sinks and countertops have been *kashered*.

- ✡ At any point, the oven can be *kashered*. Put any items to be *kashered* on the racks, if needed.

- ✡ Fire up the *kashering* pot again. *Kasher* any silverware, pots, pans, etc. in the boiling water. Be sure every inch touches the water. If needed, flip it. Unlike with *Tavelling*, items don't have to be submerged all at once.

CAN-DO KOSHER!

- ✡ As soon as it comes out of the boiling water, immerse it in very cold water. It's now kosher!
- ✡ Once all items are *kashered*, or if you have purchased any new items, take them to the *mikvah*, the beach or a lake.
- ✡ *Tavel* items before using them. It is preferable to wash them after, as outdoor *mikvaot* may have mosquito dunks.
- ✡ Start using your nice brand-new Kosher Kitchen!!!

**Now that you have done everything, *Mazal Tov* on having become completely kosher!!!
(See, I know you Can-Do it too!)**

About the Author

Chasya Katriela Eshkol is the Executive Director of a 501(c)(3) non-profit organization, called "The Yoshon Network Inc.", which helps people keep the *Mitzvah* of *Yashan*. For more information, visit Yoshon.com.

Other Books by Chasya include:

Can-Do Kosher: A Quick and Concise Guide to Becoming Kosher (First Edition 2016)

Vintage Grain: The Mitzvah of Keeping Yashan (2018)

Chasya's next book is planned to be released in 2019.

CanDoKosher.com

WriteChasya@gmail.com